MW01641518

Keys of the Kingdom
21 Day Prayer Guide to Breakthrough

For more information: info@exitoenlafamila.com

ISBN: 978-1-7334043-1-0

Keys of the Kingdom

21 Day Prayer Guide to Breakthrough

Kristen Román

Dedication

To my faithful husband Luis and my amazing sons, Josiah, Christopher, and Andrew who continually call me to greater faith no matter what the obstacles; thank you for always walking by my side.

To my incredible family, here in the United States and in Mexico; thank you for supporting me in every stage of my life.

To all the members of Viva Church International who are building God's kingdom alongside us; may this serve as a tool to equip each one of us in the task of reconciling lives to the Father.

I love you all!

Contents

The Keys

Words are powerful. Words are so powerful that the Bible tells us in Proverbs 18:21 that they can determine life and death. Most of us don't think in terms of life and death, but we all know what it feels like when something is said to us that builds us up (produces life) or tears us down (produces death). And often those words are followed by the thought: "Why did that affect me so much?" It is not that the words themselves hold some supernatural ability; they are powerful because they *access* power. Words are like keys that unlock doors to the power of life or death. It is so important to be aware of the doors we are opening in the spirit through the words we speak. In order for our words to produce life, they must be connected to truth; not the perceived truth of the moment, but the absolute truth. In Matthew 16:15-19, Jesus promised Peter that the church would be given keys that would have the ability to bind and loose, to lock or unlock.

And it is amazing that this promise came after Peter *spoke* a declaration of truth, after he *spoke* what he saw in the heavenly kingdom and not what he saw with his natural eyes. The Father opened the door to the heavenly realm and let Peter access a divine revelation — the truth that Jesus was indeed the Messiah, the Son of God.

> *It is so important to be aware of the doors we are opening in the spirit through the words we speak.*

Jesus didn't look like a savior or a divine king. The Scriptures describe Him as a simple, humble man, traveling from place to place. (Isaiah 53:2, Matthew 8:20) Peter didn't speak what he saw with his natural eyes or perceived with his five senses. He received a revelation of truth that was unseen and when he spoke this truth, he was using a key that accessed the Kingdom of God! It is important to recognize that he gained this access when he *spoke*. Jesus asked him, "Who do you *say* that I am?" He didn't ask, "Who do you *think* that I am?" Peter answered with confidence: "You are the Messiah, the son of the Living God." And what happens next is a game changer; it is the end of a chapter in history and the beginning of something entirely new!

Jesus replied: "Blessed are you Simon... for this was not revealed to you by flesh and blood, but by my Father in heaven. And I tell you that you are Peter, and on this rock I will build my church, and the gates of Hades will not overcome it. I will give you the keys of the kingdom of heaven; whatever you bind on earth will be bound in heaven, and whatever you loose on earth will be loosed in heaven." (Matthew 16:17-19)

This is a monumental declaration. Over the years, some have mistakenly interpreted this to mean that the church would be built on Peter, the literal person, and his lineage. But we learn by studying the rest of Scripture that the only firm foundation is

Jesus. The implications of Matthew 16:17 go far beyond the limitations of a mere human.

We can hear the joy and excitement in Jesus' response to Peter. In essence, He was saying: *Yes! Finally! Someone got it! And now Peter, you hold the keys! You have seen what natural eyes have not and you have declared it as truth! I am the Christ! I am the door! And through me you have access to the Father and His Kingdom! And on this access I will build my Church and the gates of Hell cannot stand against it!* And just like Peter, we can be confident that the gates of hell (kingdom of darkness) cannot overcome us as long as we are using the keys He gave us to access the kingdom of heaven! Our victory in life is directly related to which kingdom we are accessing at any given time. And I believe we choose that access

Our victory in life is directly related to which kingdom we are accessing at any given time.

through what we think and what we speak. That is why it is so important to be aware of our thoughts and words and how they affect the atmosphere around us. Romans 8:6 says:

The mind governed by the flesh is death, but the mind governed by the Spirit is life and peace.

Wow, there it is again: life and death. This time it is talking about our thoughts, which is the beginning of the life cycle of our words. Every word spoken starts as an embryonic thought. And the more we feed that thought and nurture it, the faster it grows and becomes truth in our mind. It is only a matter of time before it is birthed out of our mouth! (Luke 6:45) That is why it is so important that our minds are governed by the Spirit. And the reward for that is priceless — life and peace for ourselves and those who interact with us. We live in a crazy world that is in desperate need of peace. But as long as we are searching for peace outside of God's truth, we will not find it. The reason for this is because the same

Spirit who gives peace is the One who leads us into all truth. (John 16:13) We can't separate life and peace from absolute truth! And the absolute truth that still exists in this upside down world plagued with relativism is God's word. The Bible is the most powerful resource we have! The power of God is released in our lives when we speak the truth of His Word in faith. Yet to speak the truth, we need to know the truth; not only in our minds but in our spirits. This takes time and training. A marathon runner can study the theory of movement and strength. He can know in his mind the correct techniques and strategies, but all of that information is useless if he doesn't get up and run!

We can't separate life and peace from absolute truth!

Some people may feel daunted by just hearing the word "training" and want to quit before they even get started! The good news is that you are never alone in the process. John 8:31,32 is more than an iconic declaration of liberty. It is actually a conditional promise of freedom through relationship:

If you hold to my teaching, you are really my disciples. Then you will know the truth, and the truth will set you free. (John 8:31,32)

If we hold to His teaching, if we meditate on God's Word and if we stand firm in its precepts, then we will know the truth. And truth is not a philosophical or theological concept; truth is a person! Jesus said, *"I am the Way, the Truth and the Light and no one comes to the Father except through me."* (John 14:6) When we train our spirits in the promises of the Bible, we are not reading mere words. We are actually encountering the person of Jesus, who is the Word! And it is that same Jesus, the Truth, who sets us free! That's great news! We are not alone in this spiritual journey, striving by our own strength to do better. Jesus is with us and He is committed through His grace to complete the work that He began in our lives. He is like the trainer with the stopwatch, motivating us to get up before daylight and hit the track. Our job is simply to say to Jesus, "Lord, here I am — let's do it!"

And that's where this book comes in. It is essentially a training guide for the spirit, designed to build our faith muscles and shape our thinking and words, conforming them to the Word of God. It is based on the Scriptures and prayer declarations (prayers that agree with God's Word and are spoken out loud) that I have compiled for my own personal use. I have had many internal struggles and health challenges over the years and I have experienced amazing breakthroughs with what I am sharing with you. I know from my own life that it develops spiritual conditioning and prepares us for victory in the race! But before we get running, let's look at four of the "keys" we need to use to have an effective training time with the Lord.

Key #1

The first key is understanding the power of rightly aligned words.

James 5:16 says: "*Therefore confess your sins to each other and pray for each other so that you may be healed. The prayer of a righteous person is powerful and effective.*" The idea of righteousness in this verse is to have right standing before God. It implies the idea of being rightly "aligned". First and foremost, to have effective prayers we must be in Christ. (If you haven't yet given your life to Jesus, I suggest you see the prayer on p. 83) It is through faith in Jesus Christ that we stand righteous before God the Father, perfectly aligned with Him with no barriers between us. That is why it is so important to take care of the relationship we now have with the Father and not let sin come between us.

Secondly, for our prayers to be effective they must be properly aligned, both with the Word of God and with our own heart. Jesus says in John 15:7,

If you remain in me and my words in you, you may ask anything in my name and it will be done for you.

What an amazing promise! If we align our words with His Word, it is like placing the key in the matching lock and activating the promise of God. Yet, even if it is placed in the correct lock, it will only turn if we have faith. Something very powerful happens in the spirit when we confess with our mouth *and* believe in our heart. The agreement between heart and word is necessary for salvation (Rom. 10:9) and I believe it is also necessary for effective prayer declarations! We don't want to fall into the cycle of vain repetitions, (Matt.6:7) which is confessing without believing. And I am definitely not talking about "the name it and claim it" concept where words themselves are elevated to some magical level and seem to have a power of their own. Words become powerful when the heart connects and we believe them. And that is true for both negative and positive declarations.

Words become powerful when the heart connects and we believe them.

We see this in the natural realm as well. Children, for example, can be deeply wounded by negative words spoken over them, not because of the words themselves, but because at some point their heart connected with them and they began to believe them. Even with positive words, believing is an essential element for them to make an impact in our lives. My dear husband tells me often that I look beautiful and then gets frustrated with me, because I complain about my wrinkles and aging skin. He often exclaims, "Why don't you believe me?" His words are loving and powerful and could be life changing, but I need to believe them for there to be an effect on how I think, speak and act. I need to look in the mirror and see what he sees. The same thing is true in the spirit. Like my husband, God often exclaims: *Dear one, why don't you believe me? Why don't you believe that I have forgiven you, healed you, set you free and given you all that you need to walk in victory? Lift up your eyes and see what I see!*

Peter believed and Jesus rejoiced. Like Peter, we must see what God sees, believe it as truth and then speak it out. There is a common misconception that faith is blind, that to walk in faith is to step out in complete darkness. I do not believe that faith is blind at all. Faith sees! It sees what our natural eyes do not. It sees what the Father sees and then gives us the ability to do that very thing! (John 15:6) When we know the will of our Father, we can confidently speak it out, convinced that it will come to pass. Many people struggle with wondering if

> Faith sees what our natural eyes do not.

what they are praying is God's will or not. Well, the good news is that in this guide we will only pray what we know is His will; that way we can pray with total confidence. (I believe we can have that same confidence as we pray for all areas of life, but that is something we mature into and it is unique to personal situations. My hope for this book is that it will apply to all believers, which is why we will pray for only those things directly mentioned in the Bible.) When we are connected to the Father through Jesus and rightly aligned in His Word and in faith, then we have the confidence to approach His throne, ready to receive the reality of His promises manifest in our lives!

> *We must see what God sees, believe it as truth and then speak it out.*

Key #2

The second key is understanding the power of the atonement.

When Jesus died on the cross, the Bible says that He became the curse. What does that really mean? In Deuteronomy 28-30, God gave the people of Israel the choice to live under the blessing or the curse according to their obedience in fulfilling His law. Old Testament believers (the Jews) had to fulfill the law perfectly to avoid the curse. This was quite a task, consuming all parts of their daily lives and giving root to legalism. But when Jesus came He fulfilled the law for us, took the curse for our disobedience and triumphantly declared on the cross "It is finished!" This means we are free from ALL that was included in the punishment for breaking the law of God.

But Christ has rescued us from the curse pronounced by the law. When he was hung on the cross, he took upon himself the curse for our wrongdoing. (Galatians 3:13)

We are free from legalism, poverty, anxiety, confusion, depression, oppression, chronic sickness, death (spiritual death) and everything else that fell under the curse for breaking the law! This amazing truth must sink deep into our hearts. Most Christians understand that Jesus paid the price for their sins on the cross. And because of that we now have the promise of eternal life with Him. Thank you, God! We are so grateful for this. But most of us lack understanding about the entirety of "it is finished". The curse is broken now! That means that now we can walk in His victory every day. We can know this in our heads, but at some point it must drop into our spirits for us to be able to own it and walk in it. To not walk in this truth, I believe is an affront and offense to the cross. Christ paid a very high price for us and I don't know about you, but I don't want any part of His sacrifice to be in vain! If I only receive the provision of eternal life, but kindly decline the rest, I am minimizing the impact of His sacrifice. When He hung on the cross, ALL of the punishments of the curse came upon Him. Imagine all the sins, all the suffering and all the sickness of humanity being laid on Jesus at that moment in time — what indescribable agony:

> *It is finished: past, present, and future.*

But [in fact] He has borne our griefs, And He has carried our sorrows and pains, Yet we [ignorantly] assumed that He was stricken, struck down by God and degraded and humiliated [by Him] But He was wounded for our transgressions, He was crushed for our wickedness [our sin, our injustice, our wrongdoing]; The punishment [required] for our well-being fell on Him, And by His stripes [wounds] we are healed. (Isaiah 53:4,5 Amplified Bible)

Moments before the Son of God gave Himself to death, He cried out, "It is finished!" It is finished: past, present, and future. Period. No comma, no semi colon… period. It is finished. Our lives don't have to be defined by legalism, striving, depression, anxiety, addictions, chronic suffering, sickness and misfortune. He took all of this upon himself so we would not have to ourselves. And of course, this doesn't mean we won't have hardship and trials. We live in a fallen world and there are universal consequences to sin that sometimes intersect with our lives. But they should not be ongoing, persistent nor defining. If they are, it is a red flag to stop and ask the Holy Spirit what is going on. *Am I letting someone else's word, other than the Father's be the final word over my life? Did someone speak negative words (curses) over me that I embraced and believed? Am I letting the enemy have the upper hand through sin in my life? Have we forgiven those who have hurt us? Do I really believe that God is good and my freedom does not depend on what I do, but what He already did for me? …*

I understand that times of struggle can be intense and complicated. These questions are simply to guide us into a deeper conversation with the Holy Spirit and lead us beyond the desperate cry: "Why, God?"

Whatever the situation may be, every season of trial has something in common: the temptation to pull away from God and fall into condemnation, despair and negativity. We have an evil adversary who is out to destroy us. (John 10:10) And he will take advantage of any open door or opportunity that we give him to rob, kill and destroy our faith and trust in God. The good news is no matter what the enemy's inroad has been in our lives, we can close that door today! James 4:7 says, "*Submit yourselves then to God. Resist the devil, and he will flee from you.*" Submit and resist; both actions are of equal importance. We submit by humbling ourselves, surrendering our will to God. And we resist by deciding to walk in God's truth and not listen to the lies that hinder our faith. It is a simple biblical solution, but it is not easy. To walk in God's truth, we need to break toxic thought patterns and negative habitual responses by replacing them with God's Word. That is what the second half of this book is about. But before we move into that, we need to spend a little time understanding our authority in Him. Remember, it is the righteous person's prayer that is powerful and effective, the one in right standing, the one who knows what he has received through the sacrifice of Jesus and knows the power and authority of the sword he wields.

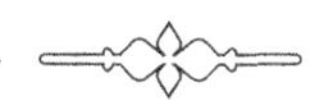

No matter what the enemy's inroad has been in our lives, we can close that door today!

Key #3

The third key is understanding the power of the believer's authority.

Jesus said that we were to do the works that He did and even greater. He was very clear that He only operated out of the authority the Father gave Him, not of His own. We are adopted into God, into His inheritance and we are given the same authority Christ had to do the works He did. This does not signify, by any means, that we are equal to Him; it is a matter of function, not identity. We are not God; we are His children. The identity is very different. But in function we are to operate as His body, healing and delivering the wounded and oppressed as He did. We are His ambassadors, issuing "passports" for His kingdom, applying His laws and representing His culture. Second Corinthians 5:19-20 makes a powerful declaration:

...That God was in Christ reconciling the world to Himself, not counting people's sins against them [but canceling them]. And He has committed to us the message of reconciliation [that is, restoration to favor with God]. So we are ambassadors for Christ, as though God were making His appeal through us; we [as Christ's representatives] plead with you on behalf of Christ to be reconciled to God. (Amplified Bible)

As His ambassadors, we represent His kingdom no matter where we are! I once read a quote by the director of the Protocol School of Washington. "When you visit an embassy, you are no longer on American soil," she said, "you are in someone else's world." I wonder if when people come in contact with me they feel as though they have entered someone else's world? That "someone" of course is my heavenly Father! Do I

> *Our prayers are backed by the most powerful governing power that exists!*

represent my Father's kingdom well and everything He represents? Do I walk in His authority, exercising His will on earth as it in heaven? The believer's authority is an ambassador's authority. An effective ambassador is in constant contact with the king or governing leader that he represents. He chooses his words carefully, because they do not express his own will, but instead the will of the one he represents.

When we pray, it is important to know who we are and whose we are.

In the same way, we must be in close contact with our King, so that our words will represent His will. That is the key to effective and powerful declarations that move the earthly realm. When we pray and declare the will of the Heavenly King, our prayers are backed by the most powerful governing power that exists! And what's more, we have the privilege of not only being ambassadors, but also heirs. Our King is not only our royal sovereign, but

Sometimes our five senses speak louder than our spirits.

He is also our loving Father. So our authority is based not only on representation, but also on birthright! We have double access. That is exciting! When we pray, it is crucially important to know who we are and whose we are. When this truth penetrates our being, we can confidently declare that our words are the will of our Father and King and that they are backed by the authority of the Kingdom of Heaven! Some of us, including myself, still need to grow in this area of "knowing". We need to grow in believing more what the Father says than what we see with our eyes or sense in our emotions or feel in our body. Sometimes our five senses speak louder than our spirits. The purpose of this book is to build our faith, to help train our thoughts and words to align with His Word and the more we speak His truth, the more our heart will believe. And when our heart and our words are aligned with His heart and His Word, the supernatural manifests in the natural!

Key # 4

The fourth key is keeping our eyes on Jesus

In Matthew 14, two chapters before Peter is promised the keys, we read about a life changing encounter that he has with Jesus walking on the water. Earlier that day, Jesus invited the disciples to take part in the miracle of the multiplication of the fish and the bread and their faith was running high. (Matthew 14:13-21) They saw natural laws being defied by the power of the One who created them. So when Peter boldly asks to walk out to Jesus on the water, I am sure he is expecting that same supernatural power of God to operate, superseding the physical laws of nature. What he was not expecting, however, was the wind: the forceful opposition to his faith. Imagine the thrill of feeling a sure foundation under his feet, as he took his first courageous steps. *Steady now!* Step by step he gets closer to the Author of this amazing story. And then the mounting panic rises as the wind picks up, drawing his eyes away from the One who beckoned him. Sinking quickly into the dark swirling sea, he cries: “Oh Lord, save me!” Jesus extends His hand and pulls him to safety, at the same time firmly reminding him that he must not doubt. In the same way, we must not doubt. So many times we see the answer to our prayers as the atmosphere begins to shift. We can see the miracle breaking through the stormy waters. Faith rises and hope comes alive – the medical report shows improvement, the struggling teenager reaches out for help, the distant spouse comes home, the failing business revives...and then the wind begins to blow. Circumstances suddenly change and it looks like things are heading back in the wrong direction.

It is in these moments that we need to keep our eyes on Jesus, focusing our thoughts on what He has already done and the progress we have already made. We are doing it! We are walking on the surface of our circumstances! We are walking on the sure foundation of His promises despite what is happening around us. That incredible sensation of a few moments of solid ground beneath our feet is all

A little connection equals a little faith which equals a little breakthrough.

we need to keep going. If we let our eyes stray and focus on what is against us instead of Who is for us, it will sink us every time. The key to maintaining a breakthrough is in the person of Jesus. Our faith is not enough and God knows that. Jesus called Peter, "You of little faith" even after he stepped out of a boat in the middle of the night, believing he could walk on water! Nobody else was stepping out. It seemed like he was the one who had great faith. I believe he did. It was that great faith that got him out of the boat and the same faith that empowered his first steps, treading on the impossible. However, his faith quickly depleted when he lost connection with the source of his faith. We can imagine it as a rechargeable battery that gets plugged into the power source to recharge. Spending a little time with Jesus and getting a fresh dose of faith is great, but a little connection equals a little faith which equals a little breakthrough. Some of us need more than a little breakthrough! What we are facing is way beyond our ability to resolve. It is a dark sea of impossibility and to walk on it we need His faith! Peter's faith was "charged up" enough to take those first steps out of the boat, but instead of plugging into Jesus to keep going, he turned his attention and connected instead to the natural circumstances. Doubt was the weight that sank him.

As we move on to the next section of this book with the declarations of faith, it is so important to remember that it is not a method or mantra. What we do or say has lasting, life-changing power only if we are connected to the power source of Jesus. The good news is that if we are believers, we have the Holy Spirit living in us — a constant connection to the power of God. Yet like Peter on the water, the connection will break and we will quickly "discharge," if we get distracted by the circumstances around us. This is especially true when we are starting to see a breakthrough. I know from my personal journey of faith, that when I feel like things are improving and I start to see in the natural what I know to be true in the spirit, often times the enemy pushes back and it looks like I am losing ground. But that is when it is most important to hold on to the words of Hebrews 12:1-2:

"Therefore, since we are surrounded by such a great cloud of witnesses, let us throw off everything that hinders and the sin that so easily entangles. And let us run with perseverance the race marked out for us, fixing our eyes on Jesus, the pioneer and perfecter of faith"

Don't be moved by the wind! Don't give up! Keep pressing forward! Stay plugged in and keep your eyes on Jesus!

The Training Plan

I recommend reading the Scriptures and prayers in the following section OUT LOUD, several times a day, because faith comes by hearing and hearing by the Word of God! (Romans 10:17, KJV)

They are divided into 21 day segments each with related scriptures and a starting prayer. The starting prayer is designed to inspire you to add your own personalized petitions and declarations. I also recommend reading the Scriptures in first person to remind yourself that God made these incredible promises thinking of you! The first two days of Scriptures have the first person pronouns in brackets to get you started.

God created our mind and knows perfectly how it works. That is why He instructs us to meditate on

His Word continually (Psalm 1: 2, Joshua 1: 8) He knows that to renew the mind we need to speak the language that our brain understands: repetition! Scientific advances have allowed us to see the wonder of His creation, showing that it takes 21 days to create a new neural pattern of thought and 63 days to solidify it, making it a more permanent way of thinking. I recommend repeating the 21 day cycle at least 3 times.

Remember the mind cannot renew the spirit, only the Spirit of God and His Word can do that. However, our spirit does have the authority to renew our mind. The idea is to renew our minds with His Word every day until faith-filled thinking becomes a life-changing habit!

* Note: For those desiring a breakthrough in health challenges, I do not recommend stopping medication without first consulting a doctor. I suggest praying that the medicine will only have a positive effect, canceling any negative side effects while your health is improving. Ideally, seek a doctor who will walk with you as you believe for the Lord's healing!

Ready - Set - Go!

Building Faith for Revelation and Authority

Day 1

2 Peter 1:3-4

His divine power has given us [me] everything we [I] need for a godly life through our [my] knowledge of him who called us [me] by his own glory and goodness.Through these he has given us [me] his very great and precious promises, so that through them you [I] may participate in the divine nature, having escaped the corruption in the world caused by evil desires.

Colossians 2:9-10

For in Christ all the fullness of the Deity lives in bodily form, and in Christ you [I] have been brought to fullness. He is the head over every power and authority.

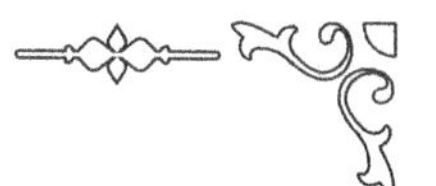

Father,

Thank You for being a good Father. Because of Your goodness, You have given me everything I need for a godly life! Everything! I thank You that I participate in the divine nature. And there is no sickness, fear, poverty, lack, strife, pride nor evil in Your nature, and likewise I refuse to have it be part of mine! I receive a greater revelation right now of who I am in You, the authority I have been given and how I am free from the evil desires of this world! I recognize that I walk in the authority given to Jesus according to Colossians 2:9. I have been brought to fullness in Him. He is the head over all power and authority and I am in Him, so I thank You God that this authority dwells in me through Your Spirit. Thank You for choosing me and equipping me to work with You in Your Kingdom. I take hold of all that the fullness entails and pray it into action in my life today that I may represent You well as I go about my day…

Building Faith for Revelation and Authority

Day 2

James 4:6-7

But He gives us [me] more grace. That is why Scripture says:"God opposes the proud, but shows favor to the humble." Submit yourselves [I submit myself], then, to God. Resist [I resist] the devil, and he will flee from you [me].

Luke 10:18-19

He replied, "I saw Satan fall like lightning from heaven. I have given you [I have been given] authority to trample on snakes and scorpions and to overcome all the power of the enemy; nothing will harm you [me]."

Father,

I stand in agreement with the truth of your Word that says the enemy has no power over me! I humble myself, submit to you God and receive revelation of my authority right now. Thank You Lord for the power to resist the enemy and I choose now to resist his lies. And as I resist and take captive my thoughts, he loses power and in fear he flees! I am now on the offensive, wielding the sword of truth in authority, trampling the enemy and all demonic forces that may come against me. NOTHING can harm me, because I am surrounded by the presence of my God, standing in His authority to overcome …

Building Faith for Revelation and Authority

Day 3

1 John 5:14-15

This is the confidence we have in approaching God: that if we ask anything according to his will, he hears us. And if we know that he hears us—whatever we ask—we know that we have what we asked of him.

Mark 11:24

Therefore I tell you, whatever you ask for in prayer, believe that you have received it, and it will be yours.

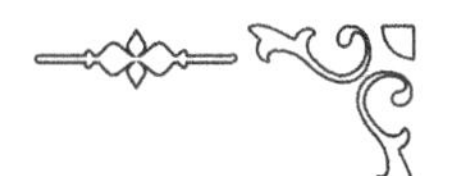

Thank You God,

You are a good Father and I can approach Your throne with confidence. I submit my desires to You and I agree with Your Word. I know that Your Word tells me that if I believe I will receive. I ask now that You strengthen my capacity to believe. I need more revelation of You and Your love to firmly believe that Your desire is to answer my prayers. I want to believe like Abraham without wavering. I want to have true faith, faith that is not moved by what I see in the natural. Forge that faith in me, Lord. I submit myself to Your will and to Your process. I speak Your Word out loud so that my spirit grows in faith because according to Romans 10:17, faith comes by hearing and hearing by the Word of God…

Building Faith for Revelation and Authority

Day 4

Matthew 18:18-19
"Truly I tell you, whatever you bind on earth will be bound in heaven, and whatever you loose on earth will be loosed in heaven. Again, truly I tell you that if two of you on earth agree about anything they ask for, it will be done for them by my Father in heaven."

John 15:7
If you remain in me and my words remain in you, ask whatever you wish, and it will be done for you.

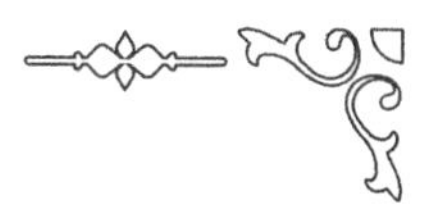

Lord,

I pray for revelation to understand the power of agreement and of binding and loosing. I come into agreement now with You God and Your purposes in my life, in my family and in the lives of those around me. I bind the powers of hell that they will not prevail in our lives. And I loose the power of heaven to work on our behalf. I choose to meditate on Your Word so that it remains alive in me and transforms my desires to align them with Your heart. I ask You Lord to make me more like You so that I can impact the lives around me with Your love…

Building Faith for Healing

Day 5

Isaiah 53:5

But he was pierced for our transgressions, he was crushed for our iniquities; the punishment that brought us peace was on him, and by his wounds we are healed.

Romans 8:1,2,6,11

Therefore, there is now no condemnation for those who are in Christ Jesus, because through Christ Jesus the law of the Spirit who gives life has set you free from the law of sin and death… The mind governed by the flesh is death, but the mind governed by the Spirit is life and peace… But if Christ is in you, then even though your body is subject to death because of sin, the Spirit gives life because of righteousness. And if the Spirit of him who raised Jesus from the dead is living in you, he who raised Christ from the dead will also give life to your mortal bodies because of his Spirit who lives in you.

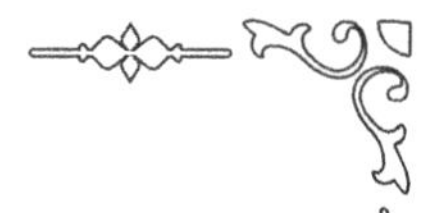

Thank You Jesus,

For having mercy on us and coming to rescue us by giving Your life on the cross. You are the Word sent to heal us. I thank You that by Your stripes I am healed, present tense, already done. I choose to receive the healing that has already been paid for by Your precious blood. I will not let Your suffering be in vain by not receiving the provision of salvation and healing You made for me. I thank You that Your Word is active in my body today. I declare that my mind is governed by the Spirit and I join my words with His and speak life over every cell in my body declaring in faith that I am healed!...

Building Faith for Healing

Day 6

Psalm 118:13-17

I was pushed back and about to fall, but the Lord helped me. The Lord is my strength and my defense; he has become my salvation. Shouts of joy and victory resound in the tents of the righteous:"The Lord's right hand has done mighty things, The Lord's right hand is lifted high; the Lord's right hand has done mighty things!" I will not die but live, and will proclaim what the Lord has done.

Psalm 107:19-20

Then they cried to the Lord in their trouble, and he saved them from their distress. He sent out his word and healed them; he rescued them from the grave.

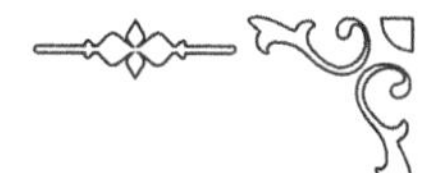

Lord,

I believe that it is Your desire to help me and rescue me. You are Faithful and True and You have done great things for Your children. I am Your beloved child and I believe You hear me when I pray. You hear my cries and as a good Father You come quickly to the rescue. I thank You that You sent Your healing Word to restore me. I stand on that Word today and I wait patiently for You Lord, patiently yet actively believing that my healing that is already a reality in the spirit realm will be manifest in the natural* and by faith I proclaim the wonders You have done…

* *Isaiah 58:8*

Building Faith for Healing

Day 7

Mark 5:30,34

At once Jesus realized that power had gone out from him... He said to her, "Daughter, your faith has healed you. Go in peace and be freed from your suffering."

Matthew 8:3

Jesus reached out and touched him. "I am willing," he said. "Be healed!" And instantly the leprosy disappeared.

Matthew 12:15

A large crowd followed him, and he healed all who were ill.

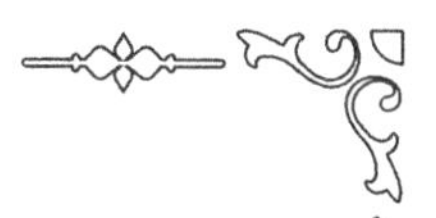

Jesus,

You are my Healer and Your power is accesible to me. I reach out and touch You now, knowing that You healed all who came to You with need. It is Your very nature and desire to heal me and I agree with Your will for my healing. I pray that my faith will be strengthened to receive my healing, that there would be no doubt or double-mindedness in me that could block Your answer.* I speak Your words prophetically over my body: Body, listen to the words of Jesus my Healer: "I am willing! Be healed! Your faith has healed you, Go in peace and be freed from your suffering!" I declare today by faith that I am set free from all infirmity and suffering, and God I praise You for doing this great work in me…

*James 1:6-8

Building Faith for Healing

Day 8

Psalm 30:1-2

I will exalt you, Lord, for you lifted me out of the depths and did not let my enemies gloat over me. Lord my God, I called to you for help, and you healed me.

Exodus 15:26

If you listen carefully to the Lord your God and do what is right in his eyes, if you pay attention to his commands and keep all his decrees, I will not bring on you any of the diseases I brought on the Egyptians, for I am the Lord, who heals you.

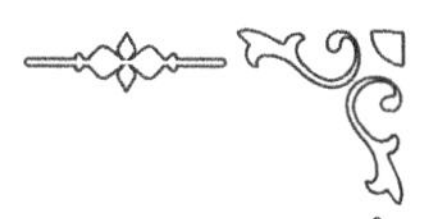

Father God,

You are so good to me. Thank You for not treating me as Your enemy, but instead You care for me as Your child. I am diligent to listen to You and do what is right in Your eyes, yet I realize that I can only keep the condition for this healing promise because of Jesus' sacrifice! He fulfilled the law for me and by His blood I stand righteous before You. Because of this I can now receive the promise of healing. I know that disease and suffering in my body do not come from Your hand. Thank You for Your protection from the gloating demonic entities sent to afflict me. I resist this affliction and I refuse anything that doesn't come from You. Today I receive my healing and restoration with full confidence that through Jesus the work is already done…

Building Faith for Healing

Day 9

Isaiah 40:29-31

He gives strength to the weary and increases the power of the weak. Even youths grow tired and weary, and young men stumble and fall; but those who hope in the Lord will renew their strength. They will soar on wings like eagles; they will run and not grow weary, they will walk and not be faint.

Psalm 103:2-5

Praise the Lord, my soul, and forget not all his benefits—who forgives all your sins and heals all your diseases, who redeems your life from the pit and crowns you with love and compassion, who satisfies your desires with good things so that your youth is renewed like the eagle's.

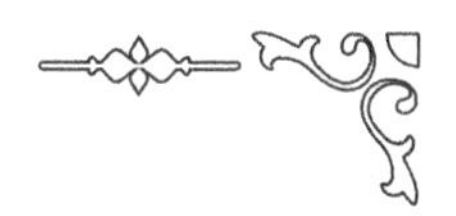

God,

How amazing it is that serving You comes with a full benefit package! Thank You for forgiving my sins AND healing all my diseases — ALL of them. There is nothing outside of the provisions You have made. I have full coverage with no exclusions! And today I am using my benefits, I submit a claim for the healing of my mind, body and emotions. I declare that even now I am receiving new strength and vitality. My youth is being renewed like the eagle, so I may soar above my circumstances and enjoy the goodness of the Lord! Praise the Lord, my soul, and all that is within me praise his Holy Name…

Building Faith for Peace and Freedom from Fear & Anxiety

Day 10

2 Timothy 1:7

For God has not given us a spirit of fear and timidity, but of power, love, and self-discipline.

Romans 8:15

The Spirit you received does not make you slaves, so that you live in fear again; rather, the Spirit you received brought about your adoption to sonship. And by him we cry, *"Abba,* Father."

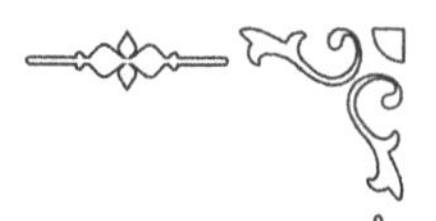

Abba,

I am so grateful that You have chosen me as Your adopted child and that You have freed me from slavery. I declare that fear is no longer my master. I receive the inheritance of my Father which is power, love and self discipline. I choose to take control of my thoughts and submit them to the Lord Jesus Christ. I will only think Your thoughts for me which are good and full of life and peace. All anxiety must leave my mind and body right now by the authority of Jesus Christ who lives in me…

Building Faith for Peace and Freedom from Fear & Anxiety

Day 11

John 14:27

I am leaving you with a gift—peace of mind and heart. And the peace I give is a gift the world cannot give. So don't be troubled or afraid.

Isaiah 26:3

You will keep in perfect peace those whose minds are steadfast, because they trust in you.

Jesus,

I decide to open the gift of peace that You have given me by setting my mind on You. This beautiful gift was costly and I will not take it for granted by walking in fear and worry. I recognize that I must choose to be steadfast in my thoughts and not let anxiety rule me. I choose to trust You Lord. I take my thoughts captive according to 2 Cor. 10:5 and bring them under the lordship of Christ. I will not let my thoughts wander into catastrophic and pessimistic outcomes. Your plans for me are good* and I close the door to all thoughts that are not in line with Your promise of peace and wellbeing. . .

* Jeremiah 29:11

Building Faith for Peace and Freedom from Fear & Anxiety

Day 12

Psalm 34:4
I sought the Lord, and he answered me; he delivered me from all my fears.

1 John 4:18
There is no fear in love. But perfect love drives out fear, because fear has to do with punishment. The one who fears is not made perfect in love.

Lord,

I need more of your love. I recognize that if I fear the solution is not to have more courage, but to have more love! When I soak in Your love, I become more aware of Your power and goodness and less aware of my weakness. I seek You Lord today and I know that You deliver me from all evil. I wrap myself in your love and declare that I am free from fear. I recognize that fear is a counterfeit prophetic spirit that predicts negative scenarios over my life, and I cancel those predictions now and prophesy the true Word of the Lord which is a long and prosperous life.* …

*Deut. 5:33, 3 John 2, Psalm 9:16

Building Faith for Peace and Freedom from Fear & Anxiety

Day 13

Deuteronomy 31:8

Do not be afraid or discouraged, for the Lord will personally go ahead of you. He will be with you; he will neither fail you nor abandon you.

Isaiah 41:10

So do not fear, for I am with you; do not be dismayed, for I am your God. I will strengthen you and help you; I will uphold you with my righteous right hand.

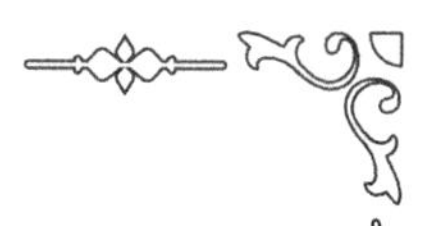

Lord,

You have commanded me not to fear, it is not a suggestion; it is an order. I understand You would never tell me to do something that You have not given me the ability to do. Thank you for reminding me that I am able to live without fear and the strength to do that comes from You! You have promised to help me and to personally walk ahead of me to light the way. I will not fear because I am not alone. Your rod and Your staff guide me and comfort me! If You are with me, who can be against me?* I know that in my weakness Your strength is made perfect in me. Like David in Psalm 34, I speak to my soul: Soul, do not be discouraged for the Lord is with me! Body, do not be anxious because the Lord is with me. Let all my being submit to the Word of the Lord: Do not fear!...

* Psalm 23:4, Romans 8:31

Building Faith for Trust and Protection

Day 14

Proverbs 18:10
The name of the Lord is a high tower; the righteous run into it and are safe.

Psalm 46:1
God is our refuge and strength, always ready to help in times of trouble.

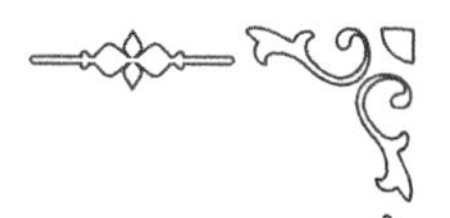

God,

You are my refuge, I run into You and I am safe. I know that You are always with me, but I also know that I must seek your manifest presence. You are always there Lord ready to help, but I must take action to run to Your protection and surround myself with Your name. I turn my affection to You now and seek Your presence. I choose not to put my confidence in my own strength, ability and resources. I run into that safe place and take refuge in your dwelling. I pray the name of Jesus and the blood of Jesus over my life, my body, my mind and my family right now, declaring that we are surrounded by Your protection. We are safe and no harm can come to us! …*

*Psalm 27:4

Building Faith for Trust and Protection

Day 15

2 Thess. 3:3

But the Lord is faithful, and he will strengthen you and protect you from the evil one.

Exodus 14:13-14

Do not be afraid. Stand firm and you will see the deliverance the Lord will bring you today. The Egyptians you see today you will never see again. The Lord will fight for you; you need only to be still.

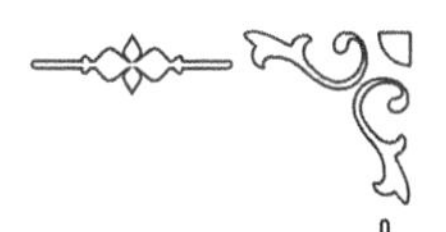

Father,

I obey Your Word and choose not to fear. You command us to be courageous; it is a decision. I bring worry and fear under Your authority and choose to trust Your protection over my life. You have promised to never leave me and that You would fight my battles. I stand firm in Your faithfulness, letting nothing move me. My emotions will not dominate me. Fear will not control me. I trust You and declare that Your voice is louder and clearer than my emotions. You have spoken to me to be still and You will fight for me. In quietness and trust is my strength* and I can rest in Your care for me. You strengthen and protect me, for You have hemmed me in on all sides and Your hand upon me keeps me safe *…

*Isaiah 30:15 , Psalm 139:5

Building Faith for Trust and Protection

Day 16

Psalm 121:7-8
The Lord will keep you from all harm—he will watch over your life; the Lord will watch over your coming and going both now and forevermore.

Psalm 91: 1,2,14-16
Whoever dwells in the shelter of the Most High will rest in the shadow of the Almighty. I will say of the Lord, "He is my refuge and my fortress, my God, in whom I trust."… "Because he loves me," says the Lord, "I will rescue him; I will protect him, for he acknowledges my name. He will call on me, and I will answer him; I will be with him in trouble, I will deliver him and honor him. With long life I will satisfy him and show him my salvation."

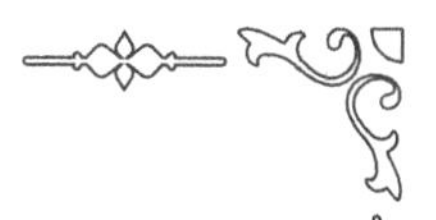

Father,

Your heart is to protect and watch over Your children. I decide to dwell in Your house today, under Your shelter and protection. I remain in Your presence by focusing my thoughts on Your goodness and not allowing anything to rob my peace. Psalm 118:9 says, "It is better to take refuge in the Lord than to trust in princes." I will not trust in the systems or authorities of this world to be my answer. You have the final word in my life. And I trust that You will guide me to any of the resources I may need. I trust You. I thank You that today You watch over my coming and going and You will keep me from harm. I go about my day in peace knowing that You have set Your angels about me. I agree with Your Word that promises that I will live a long and satisfied life…

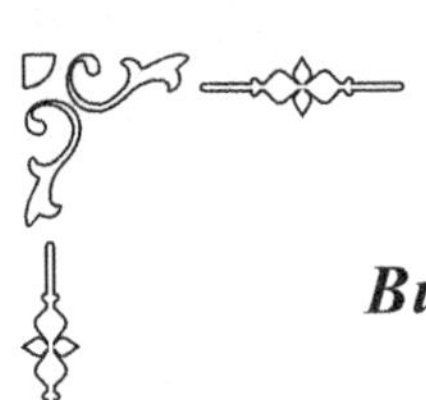

Building Faith for Provision

Day 17

Matthew 7:7-11

Keep on asking, and you will receive what you ask for. Keep on seeking, and you will find. Keep on knocking, and the door will be opened to you. For everyone who asks, receives. Everyone who seeks, finds. And to everyone who knocks, the door will be opened. You parents—if your children ask for a loaf of bread, do you give them a stone instead? Or if they ask for a fish, do you give them a snake? Of course not! So if you sinful people know how to give good gifts to your children, how much more will your heavenly Father give good gifts to those who ask him.

Romans 8:32

He who did not spare his own Son, but gave him up for us all—how will he not also, along with him, graciously give us all things?

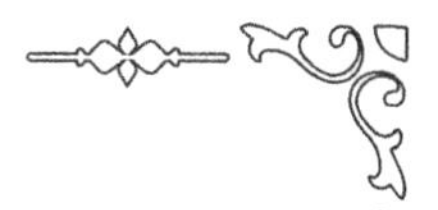

Father,

Here I am knocking once again, persisting in faith and believing that You are a good Father who desires to give Your children good gifts. I don't need to beg or convince You. I come simply to ask You to do the work in me to receive. I pray against and bind any obstacles within me or outside of me that could detain my provision. I posture myself as Your child to receive from You and I speak to my spirit to be expectant! I declare, fully trusting, that my good Father has heard me and provision is on the way! I choose now to rest in confidence that I am cared for and I choose to remember all the ways You have been faithful and I thank You…

Building Faith for Provision

Day 18

Proverbs 3:9-10

Honor the Lord with your wealth, with the first-fruits of all your crops; then your barns will be filled to overflowing, and your vats will brim over with new wine.

Luke 6:38

Give, and it will be given to you. A good measure, pressed down, shaken together and running over, will be poured into your lap. For with the measure you use, it will be measured to you.

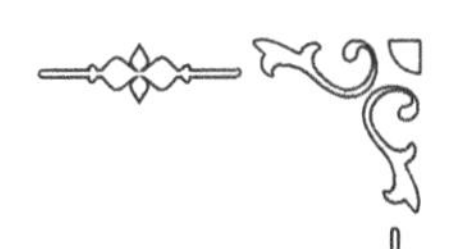

Lord,

I come to You now in submission to Your Word. Your promises are real and trustworthy. You are a good God who supplies our needs and You have promised to supply them in abundance. As I give, I declare that a poverty mentality is broken off my life! I choose to trust You and honor You with the resources I have received. I declare that I have more than enough to fulfill my needs and also to give to others. I thank You that I have the opportunity to participate with You in Your kingdom by giving, reflecting the nature of my good Father. Show me Lord how I may commit the "first-fruits" to You and honor You with the resources You have graciously entrusted to me …

Building Faith for Provision

Day 19

Philippians 4:19
But my God shall supply all your needs according to his riches in glory by Christ Jesus.

2 Cor. 9:7-8
Each of you should give what you have decided in your heart to give, not reluctantly or under compulsion, for God loves a cheerful giver. And God is able to bless you abundantly, so that in all things at all times, having all that you need, you will abound in every good work

Yes, God!

You are God of the overflow. You are the God of abundance. You supply our needs according to Your ability and Your riches in glory, not by my limitations. You are not bound by earthly economies or human error. I thank You that I am free from past mistakes. I receive Your forgiveness in areas where I have failed and dishonored You in my financial decisions and attitudes. Examine my heart Lord and align it with Yours so I may joyfully give and receive Your blessings in return. I thank You that as You provide for me I am empowered to do the good works that You have prepared in advance for me* …

*Ephesians 2:10

Building Faith for Victory and Freedom

Day 20

2 Cor. 5:17
This means that anyone who belongs to Christ has become a new person. The old life is gone; a new life has begun!

1 John 5:4
For everyone born of God overcomes the world. This is the victory that has overcome the world, even our faith. Who is it that overcomes the world? Only the one who believes that Jesus is the Son of God.

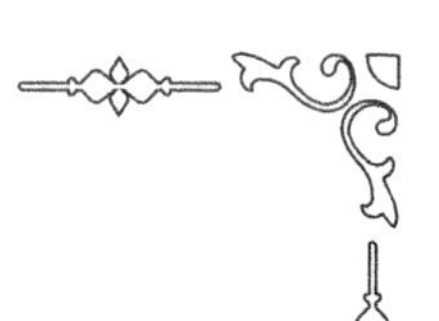

Jesus,
I believe that You are the Son of God. I thank You that with that confession of faith I receive keys to overcome the powers of darkness*. Sin no longer has a hold on me. I am not who I used to be, for You have made all things new. I declare that everyday I am becoming more like You. I may slip and fall, but I get up again and run towards the mark that You have set before me.* I will not settle for second best. I fix my eyes on You and refuse to be distracted by temptations around me. I recognize that I am Your beloved child; I have been born again, born of God, no longer under the curse, but instead under the blessing and inheritance of my Heavenly Father! I know that this world is full of affliction and my faith will be tested,* but I choose to remain steadfast, to declare my victory in You and come out stronger on the other side!...

*Matthew 16:18-19, Proverbs 24:16, 1Peter 1:7

Building Faith for Victory and Freedom

Day 21

John 8:34-36

Jesus replied, "Very truly I tell you, everyone who sins is a slave to sin. Now a slave has no permanent place in the family, but a son belongs to it forever. So if the Son sets you free, you will be free indeed."

Galatians 4:6-7

Because you are his sons, God sent the Spirit of his Son into our hearts, the Spirit who calls out, *"Abba*, Father." So, you are no longer a slave, but God's child; and since you are his child, God has made you also an heir.

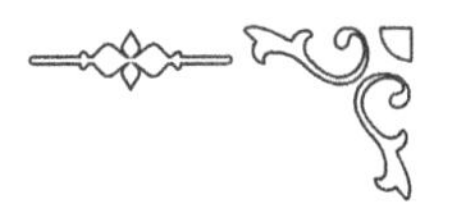

Thank You God!

I am no longer a slave to anyone or in bondage to anything. I am Your precious child and I belong to You forever. Jesus paid the price for my freedom and I believe that it is finished! Done! Truly, I am free. I don't need to feel it; I just need to believe and walk in it. Thank You Lord that I am free! Free to walk in peace and joy. Free to walk in health and wellbeing. Free to walk in prosperity and long life. Free to walk in power and authority. Free to walk in purpose and fulfillment. Free to walk out of debt and poverty. Free to walk without addictions or strongholds. Free to walk in love and healthy relationships, Free to…

Congratulations!

You finished 21 days of being connected to Jesus through His Word! I am sure that your faith muscles are already stronger, and your mind has received new revelation. Also, you now have new neural pathways in your brain, so take good care of them! Be watchful of what enters your mind and leaves your mouth! Never forget that you are a new creation in Christ. The old has passed and all things are made new! Put on the new every day, renewing your mind in His truth. (Colossians 3:1-17) The road ahead is full of challenges, but the reward of walking in faith is greater than any sacrifice. And remember that you will never be alone in the journey. Keep moving forward, consistently applying His Word in your life and you will surely see the wonders of the Lord!

We fix our eyes on Jesus, the pioneer and perfecter of faith.

"Therefore, since we are surrounded by such a great cloud of witnesses, let us throw off everything that hinders and the sin that so easily entangles. And let us run with perseverance the race marked out for us, fixing our eyes on Jesus, the pioneer and perfecter of faith..."

(Hebrews 12:1-2)

Receiving salvation and new life is as simple as praying a humble and sincere prayer to God. Jesus did the hard part with His sacrifice on the cross! The prayer below is an example of how to pray to give your life to Jesus:

Lord Jesus,
I believe that You are the Son of God and You came to give up Your life on the cross to pay the price for sin and open the way to the Father. I believe that You are my Savior and my Lord. I repent of all that I have done that has brought separation between You and me. (Take a few minutes to let the Holy Spirit bring specific situations to mind and then give each memory to Him, receiving His forgiveness.) *I receive Your forgiveness for my sins and healing in every broken place of my life. I receive eternal life that begins from this moment on. I receive the fullness of the Holy Spirit and all the gifts He has for me to grow in truth and faith. In the name of Jesus I pray, Amen.*

How exciting! The Bible says that now your name is written in the Book of Life and that you are a new creation, born again in Christ Jesus. It is very important to find a healthy Christian community to continue growing in the faith. For more information: www.myvivachurch.com

*Rom. 10:9, Luke 10:20, Rev. 3:5, 2 Cor. 5:17, John 3:3

Personal Prayers

My Prayer

His Answer

My Prayer

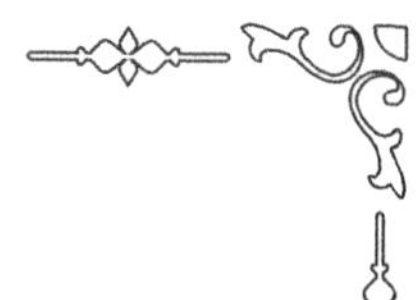

His Answer

My Prayer

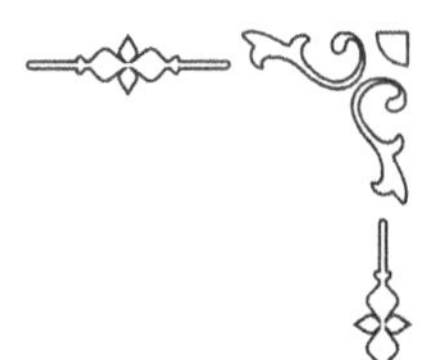

His Answer

My Prayer

His Answer

My Prayer

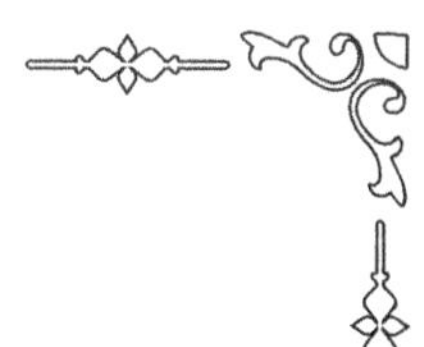

His Answer

My Prayer

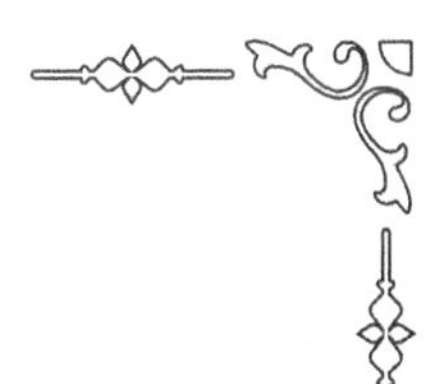

His Answer

My Prayer

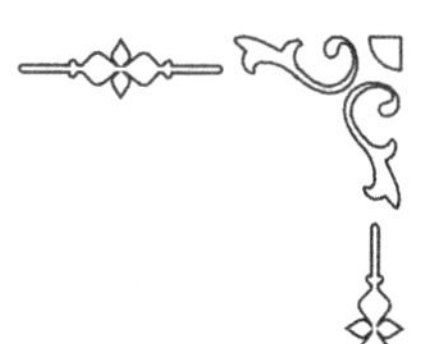

His Answer

My Prayer

His Answer

Made in the USA
Coppell, TX
17 February 2026